Bugs, Snakes and Creepy Things

And Seven Other Stories Of the Unusual

Written by Annie Mueser

A Pal Paperback from:
Xerox Education Publications
Middletown, Connecticut 06457

Copyright © 1980 Xerox Corporation. Publishing, Executive and Editorial Offices: Xerox Education Publications, 245 Long Hill Road, Middletown, Conn. 06457. Subscription Offices: Education Center, Columbus, Ohio 43216. Printed in U.S.A. XEROX is a trademark of XEROX CORPORATION. All rights reserved. Material in this book may not be reproduced in whole or in part in any format without special permission from the publisher.

ISBN 8374-3560-9

CONTENTS

Bugs, Snakes, and Creepy Things	5
The Dog Who Didn't Understand	18
Anyone Can Fall	26
Monkey in the Driver's Seat	36
Worth His Weight in...	49
Before the Earth Moved	60
Star of the Show	72
Dan's Big Dance *By Steven Otfinoski*	81

Foreword

MANY OF the stories in this book are completely true just the way we've written them. Some of them contain true facts, but made-up characters and conversations. But all of them *could* have happened.

"Bugs, Snakes and Creepy Things" is fictional, but people like Jim Robertson do work in Hollywood. They supply TV and moviemakers with strange and unusual animals.

"Anyone Can Fall" and "Star of The Show" are both about real persons and their animals.

"Before the Earth Moved" is fiction, but scientists say it is true that dogs and other animals do sense natural disasters before they actually happen.

Fact or fiction, we hope you enjoy reading all eight of these stories of the unusual.

Bugs, Snakes, And Creepy Things

"THIS IS IT," said Rita to her brother Randy, as they drove up to the small building in Burbank, California.

"Are you sure you want to go through with this?" said Randy.

Rita turned and looked at Randy. "Do you want to have a great Halloween party or not?" she asked him.

"Is it true you can get a person any kind of animal?" asked Rita.

"Of course I do," answered her brother. "I just think we may be going a little too far, that's all."

"Don't be such a coward," Rita said, getting out of the car. Randy sighed and followed her into the building.

"Are you Mr. Robertson?" Rita asked a man behind a desk.

"Yes," replied the man. "What can I do for you?"

"Is it true you can get a person any kind of animal?" asked Rita.

Jim Robertson smiled. "If it's an *unusual* animal I can get it," he answered. "I don't handle anything as ordinary as dogs or cats, or even horses. What kind of animals were you looking for?"

"Things that crawl," said Randy. "Things that slide. Things that fly."

"You'll have to be a little more exact than that," laughed Jim Robertson. "A lot of animals crawl and slide and fly."

"My brother means we want snakes and spiders and bats," said Rita. "We want them for our Halloween party."

"Sounds like some party," said Robertson. "Why don't we go into my office. We can talk about this further there."

He led them down a hall and into a room. It was Robertson's office. On the walls were many pictures of different movies. Randy pointed at one picture. It was from a horror movie.

"That was a great movie," said Randy. "I just saw it on TV last week. Was it scary!"

"I'm glad you liked it so much," said Robertson. "I was the person who got the birds together for the director. He said he wanted hundreds of fierce birds for the movie."

"Where did you find the birds?" asked Rita.

"I teased them with a piece of cheese..."

"Near the water," answered Robertson. "I collected 500 seagulls for the director. He was happy with every last one of them."

Rita pointed at another picture. "Wasn't that on television?" she asked. "I think I saw the show."

"You probably did," said the animal man. "It was one of the toughest jobs I've had. The producers of the show wanted a mouse race on the show. It was easy getting the mice. Making them run through was another story."

"How did you get them to race?" Randy wanted to know.

"I teased them with a piece of cheese," answered Robertson. "When they chased the cheese, they were racing."

"That's great!" said Rita, who was forgetting why they had come. "What other tough jobs with animals have you had?"

Jim Robertson pointed to another pic-

"We had to supply 10,000 bees..."

ture on the wall—one of a large swarm of bees. "That picture is from a TV movie," he said. "That was *the* toughest job I've ever had."

"Did you get stung?" asked Rita.

"No," smiled Robertson. "That's why it was so tough. We had to supply 10,000 bees and each bee had to have its stinger taken out. Many people had to help. Each person got a box of 100 bees at a time to work on. The workers wore gloves. They used small tweezers to pull out each stinger."

"That must have taken forever!" exclaimed Randy.

"It seemed like it," replied Robertson.

"What is the easiest job you ever had?" asked Rita.

"One customer wanted some fleas and ticks for an ad," recalled Robertson. "I just called a friend. He raises dogs. He told me to come over and help myself. I got all the fleas and ticks I needed."

Rita and Randy laughed at that story.

"This is fun telling you about my work," continued Robertson. "But aren't we forgetting why you're here? To get all those crawly things for your Halloween party?"

"Right," said Rita. "How much do you think they'll cost?"

"That all depends on how many animals you want," he replied. "Say, a couple dozen of each?"

Randy gasped. "Two dozen spiders, snakes, and bats?!" he cried.

"I don't think we'll need that many," said Rita weakly.

"OK," said Robertson. "Let me call a friend of mine and see what he's got." He picked up the telephone on his desk and dialed a number.

"Hello, Charlie?" said the animal man into the phone. "It's Jim Robertson.

Listen, I need some animals. What kind of spiders do you have on hand? Oh, hold on a second and I'll find out."

He put his hand over the receiver and turned to the two young people. "Charlie wants to know if you want poisonous spiders."

"Oh, no!" cried Rita. "Only non-poisonous ones. We don't want anyone to get bitten!"

"Then you're only inviting friends to this Halloween party?" Robertson asked.

"Definitely!" replied Randy.

"Now, how about these snakes you want," continued the animal man. "How long do you want them—six feet, seven feet?"

"Seven feet!" cried Rita.

"Charlie's got a nice nine-foot long python you could have real cheap."

Rita looked at Randy and Randy looked at Rita. "Mr. Robertson... I'd

"Charlie's got a nice nine-foot-long python."

better talk to my brother alone a moment first before we go ahead any further with picking out the animals."

"Fine, I'll tell Charlie we'll call him back later."

"Good idea," said Randy, who quickly followed his sister back down the hall.

But the two young people didn't talk. They ran down the stairs and back out to their car.

"Nine foot snakes! Poisonous spiders!" exclaimed Rita. "We must have been crazy to want to get *live* creepy things for our Halloween party!"

"*You* must have been crazy," corrected her brother. "I *never* liked the idea."

"All right," said Rita, "you don't have to rub it in. Anyone can make a mistake. Let's go to the five-and-ten cents store."

"What for?" asked Randy.

"To buy some rubber snakes, spiders and bats," replied Rita. "Those are the

BUGS, SNAKES AND CREEPY THINGS

only safe creepy things to have at a Halloween party."

Randy started up the car and they drove off. Jim Robertson watched them leave through his office window. He smiled and went back to work.

The Dog Who Didn't Understand

FOUR NEW WATCHDOGS were sent by truck to an army base in Texas. As soon as they reached the base, they were put behind a large fence. The gate was closed tight. These dogs did not look friendly. They barked and growled when anyone came near. They needed training.

THE DOG WHO DIDN'T UNDERSTAND

"These dogs look pretty wild," said John to his friend Rob. John and Rob were soldiers stationed at the base.

"That one over in the corner is the worst," said Rob. "He looks mean. Look at him. He just growls. His teeth are pretty sharp. I wouldn't want to get any closer."

Each dog was turned over to a trainer. It was the trainer's job to work with the dog and teach him what to do. The trainer who got the mean dog called the animal Rex.

Three of the dogs learned quickly. They followed the trainers. They stopped on command. They learned to obey all orders. They did just what they were told.

But Rex didn't learn quickly. He didn't seem to learn at all. Sometimes he seemed scared. He'd hide in the corner of the yard. Then he'd leap out with his sharp

"I don't know what they're going to do with Rex..."

teeth showing. He growled. He wouldn't listen.

"I don't know what they're going to do with Rex," said John one day in the yard. "Pete is supposed to train that dog, but he can't even get near him."

"I know," said Rob. "Pete was showing me the marks on his leg last night. Rex bit him twice last week."

"I heard that they might have to kill the dog," said John. "The army won't keep feeding an animal that's dangerous. The dog is of no use."

"It's too bad," said Rob. "Rex looks good from a distance. I wish someone could train him. It would be terrible to destroy an animal like that."

"There's really no choice," said John. "What else can they do? Rex bites everyone. He just doesn't obey."

"It's really strange," said Rob. "The other three are good. I wonder why Rex is so bad."

"What do you think, Angelo?" asked John. "You haven't said a word yet. You had some dogs at home. Tell us what you'd do with this one?"

"I'd give the dog another chance," said Angelo. "I'd be nice to him. He's a fine dog."

"Nice to him?" asked John. "Even if he tried to bite you?"

"Maybe he doesn't understand," said Angelo. "Maybe the dog doesn't know English. I know what that's like. My teachers used to tell me to do things. When I didn't do what they wanted, they thought I was bad. I just didn't understand."

"A dog can bite in any language," said Rob. "There's no way I'd go near that animal. I wouldn't care if he barked in French!"

The next day, Angelo talked to the

Angelo went inside the gate.... The dog bared his teeth and he growled.

dog's trainer. "Let me have a chance with Rex," he said. "I'll work with him. I'm not afraid."

"You're taking your life in your hands," Pete said. "This dog bites. He bites for real. I think he could even be a killer. He's one unhappy dog."

"Maybe so," answered Angelo. "But I'd like to give it a try. What do I have to lose?"

"Just a few pieces of your body," laughed Pete. "You are really crazy. But go ahead, and good luck."

Angelo went inside the gate. Rex ran at him. The dog bared his teeth and he growled. Then Angelo began to speak softly to the dog. No one could hear what Angelo was saying. But the dog could, and that was what counted.

The dog came closer. He ran right up to Angelo. Angelo bent down toward the dog. The dog opened his mouth.

THE DOG WHO DIDN'T UNDERSTAND

"Oh no," said Rob to Pete and John. The three of them were watching from outside the gate. "Good-bye, Angelo."

Rex came right up to Angelo. They looked each other in the eye. Angelo spoke to the dog in Spanish. He told the dog to sit. And the dog sat. He told the dog to lie down. And the dog did. He gave one order after another. Each thing he said was in Spanish. The dog did just what Angelo told him to do.

"I think Angelo has just worked a miracle," said Pete. "When I got that close to the dog, I ended up with a bloody leg."

"Hey, Angelo!" called Rob. "How did you do it? What's your secret?"

"Easy," said Angelo. "Poor Rex just didn't understand English. He must have been raised in a Spanish family. He's used to Spanish. I just happen to speak his language, that's all."

Anyone Can Fall

EVERY FOUR YEARS, many of the world's great athletes enter the Olympic Games. One of the most exciting Olympic sports is cross-country jumping. In this event, horses and riders try to get around a very tough course. The jumps are high and wide. There is a long way to gallop between the jumps. It takes a great horse and rider to do it. Many don't finish the course at all.

ANYONE CAN FALL

In the 1976 Olympics, in Canada, the cross country event was very hard. There were 36 fences on the course. Some of the world's best horses and riders were there to give it a try.

A young woman was taking her turn. She was riding a horse named Goodwill. Lots of people were watching this event. There were people all along the course and thousands more were watching it on television. Anne's mother stood near the second fence. She was happy when her daughter and Goodwill jumped it well.

The people watched carefully as Anne rode along. They cheered her as she cleared each jump. Goodwill was going well for his rider. They leaped fence number 17, then number 18. They were headed for number 19. It was a hard fence—rails over a wide, deep ditch.

As Goodwill galloped toward the fence, he stepped onto a soft spot. Just as he began to jump, he slid. His back legs crossed as he took off. He hit the fence and turned upside down. Anne fell off. She must have hit her head. She was a bit dizzy.

People hurried to help the fallen rider. She tried to get up. They told her to rest, but she got up anyway. "I see no reason why I shouldn't go on," she said.

Anne's trainer was one of those who rushed to her side. "You must not go on," he said. "Take care of yourself. You should not continue. You might really get hurt."

Anne wouldn't listen to him. She was going to get back on her horse and finish the course. "I'm off—so give me a leg up," Anne said firmly. All she wanted was a bit of help to get back on the horse.

Her trainer knew that Anne meant it. If he hadn't helped her, she would have found someone else. So, he helped her

People hurried to help the fallen rider.

into the saddle. He wished her well. Then he worried. Goodwill and his rider—still dizzy—galloped off.

Later Anne told her friends, "I don't remember anything about it. I don't remember saying any of that."

They told her how well Goodwill had jumped the last 17 fences. He hadn't touched any of them. He finished the course perfectly. Anne didn't remember any of it. She had hurt her head. She finished the course, but she didn't remember doing it.

Anne was a rider who wouldn't give up. She had always been that way. One of her first event horses was named Purple Star. He was a good horse. At least he was most of the time. He was able to jump any fence. But sometimes he didn't feel like jumping, so he just stopped. It was a dangerous habit.

In one event, Purple Star was going

...Goodwill... finished the course perfectly.

well for Anne. He galloped on and he jumped nicely. Then he got to one fence. Lots of people were looking at him and his rider. Purple Star looked back at them. He didn't jump the fence. He was too busy looking at the people. The horse stopped in his tracks, but Anne didn't stop. She went sailing over the fence without him.

"He didn't mean any harm," Anne said after the fall. "He just wanted the people to have a better look at him."

Another one of Anne's horses was named Doublet. He may very well have been her best. She loved that horse very much. Anne and Doublet had great success in events. They won the European championship together.

Doublet and Anne did have one bad fall. The horse got up and seemed to be all right. So no one worried about him. Nothing seemed wrong. But something was wrong. Doublet had hurt himself. There was a hidden break on one of his legs.

One day Anne was out riding Doublet. She heard an awful sound. It was Doublet's bad leg breaking. She got off the horse. There was nothing she could do. They had to destroy the horse. It's very hard to mend a horse's broken leg. Killing the horse is the kindest thing to do. Anne shed many tears over the loss of Doublet.

Anne didn't give up. She had lost a favorite animal, but she kept on. She tried new horses. And Goodwill was still going well for her. But horse events can be quite dangerous. And every now and then, Anne would fall off.

Anne's fall in the 1976 Olympics made her very sad. She had hoped to do better. Many people saw her fall and many of them had cameras. Her picture as she hit the ground was in newspapers all over the world. No one would let Anne forget that

Her picture as she hit the ground was in newspapers all over the world.

ANYONE CAN FALL

fall.

Why would a fall from a horse be front-page news? Anyone can fall off a horse. But Anne wasn't just anyone. She was a real princess. And her mother—the woman watching at fence number two—was Elizabeth II, the Queen of England.

Anne didn't give up. The people with the cameras didn't upset her. She was used to them. She hoped that next time they would catch her winning the event.

"Sometimes I get the feeling," she once said, "that they enjoy seeing me fall. But anyone can fall." Even a princess.

Monkey in The Driver's Seat

The phone rang in the Barnes house. Mr. Barnes picked it up on the first ring. He was upset. His daughter Connie had taken the family car to go shopping. It was the first time she had even driven alone and now she was late.

"Hello! Is that you, Connie?" asked Mr. Barnes.

"Yes, Dad," answered his daughter. Her voice sounded as if she had been crying.

"Where are you?" asked her father.

"I'm at the police station," said Connie, starting to sob. "The police won't believe me. They want you to come down here right away."

"What won't they believe?" Mr. Barnes demanded. "Connie, what's happened? Are you hurt? Is the car OK?"

"I'm all right and so is the car," explained Connie. "They stopped me because I didn't keep in my lane. That's all. But I couldn't drive in a straight line when I saw the..." Connie's words were lost in sobs.

"Take it easy, dear," said her father. "Calm down. I'll be right there. And no matter what, don't answer any more questions until I get there."

Mr. Barnes got the keys for the other

car and ran out the door. He was at the police station in ten minutes. He parked the car and ran inside.

Connie was sitting on a hard, wooden chair. She had stopped crying, but looked scared. The police officer at the desk looked anything but friendly.

"I'm very sorry, Mister Barnes," said the officer. "One of my men brought your daughter in. He stopped her because she didn't stay in her lane. She was weaving her car all over the road. He would've just given her a ticket. But when she gave him this story about why—"

"What story?" interrupted Mr. Barnes. "What story did she tell you? Why are you holding my daughter here?"

The officer sighed deeply and got up and walked around the room. "I've been a cop for fifteen years, Mister Barnes; I've heard a lot of crazy stories. But what your daughter just told me is the craziest

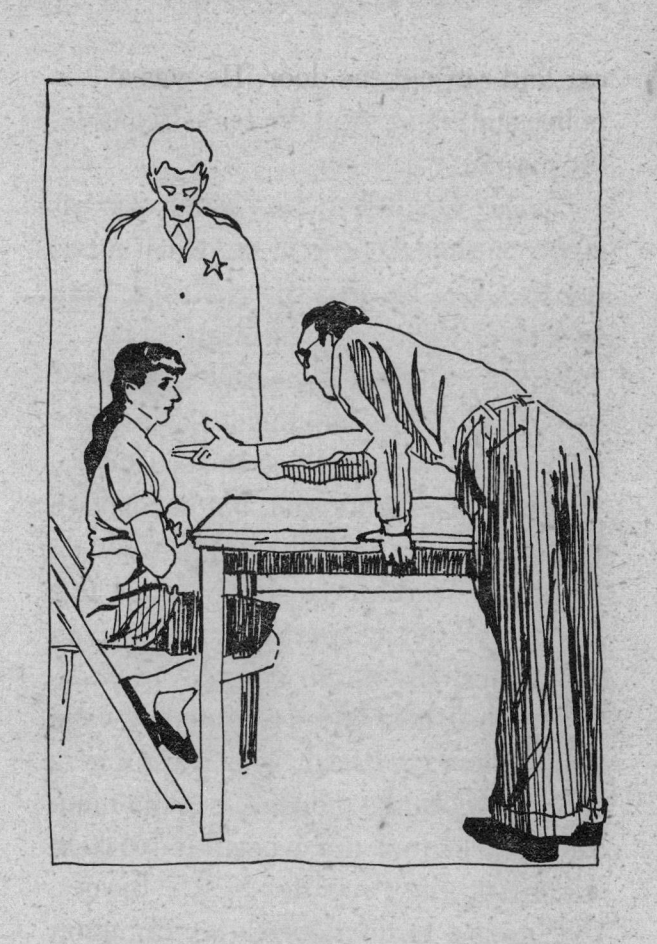

"But it's true, Dad... Honest it is!"

story of them all."

"But it's true, Dad," pleaded Connie. "Honest it is!"

"Your daughter," continued the officer, "claims the reason she went out of her lane was because she saw something in the car next to her that startled her."

"Well, what did she say she saw?" asked Mr. Barnes impatiently.

"A monkey," answered the officer.

"That's a little unusual, but not enough to affect someone's driving."

"Yes, but your daughter claims this monkey wasn't just *in* the car," explained the officer, "he was *driving* it!"

"It's the truth!" cried Connie. "It was a little yellow sports car. There was a man sitting next to the monkey, but the monkey was behind the wheel. It was the weirdest thing I ever saw."

Connie's father looked his daughter straight in the eye. "Young lady," he said

"I think you can take your daughter home."

softly, "I brought you up to always tell the truth. Now don't be afraid. Just tell me what really happened."

"But that *is* what happened!" cried Connie. "I thought my own father would believe me at least!"

Mr. Barnes looked at the police officer and shook his head sadly. "I want to believe you, Connie, but when you tell such a wild story, how can I?"

"Mister Barnes," said the officer, "I think you can take your daughter home. We won't hold her. But I'm afraid we will have to take away her driver's license for thirty days."

"But I wasn't lying. I swear it!"

"All right," said Mr. Barnes. "We won't talk anymore about it. Not now anyway."

Suddenly they came up to a red traffic light. The light turned green, but the car ahead of them didn't move.

Mr. Barnes hit his horn. A man in the passenger's seat turned around and waved. Sitting next to the man was a—monkey!

"That's the car!" cried Connie. At that same moment, the sports car started up and moved. The monkey was driving it! Mr. Barnes couldn't believe his eyes.

"Now do you believe me?" asked Connie.

"Yes!" cried her father. He stayed right behind the other car.

"I wonder where they're going?" Connie said.

"I don't know," answered Mr. Barnes, "but we're going to get to the bottom of this if we have to follow them to the state line!"

Mile after mile they followed the yellow sports car. Finally, it pulled into a circus. The car ahead stopped and so did Mr. Barnes' car.

The monkey was driving it! Mr. Barnes couldn't believe his eyes.

"Hello there!" cried the man, getting out of the sports car. "You like the way my little Chico drives, heh?" He was very large and had a small, black beard.

"How does he do it?" asked Connie.

"Well, we cheat a little," said the man with a smile. "Chico really only does the steering. I control the brakes and the gas pedal from my side. I had the car built specially that way. Chico still does pretty good though, huh?"

"He's great," agreed Mr. Barnes, "but his driving cost my daughter her license for thirty days."

A dark look came across the man's face. "I'm afraid I don't understand," he said.

Connie and her father explained what had happened earlier. When they were finished the man shook his head. "This is all Chico's and my fault," he said. "So we will be the ones to fix things up with the police. I'll call them right now and ex-

"OK," said the man with a smile. "... Come on, Chico, we're going to the police station...."

plain everything."

"Excuse me," said Mr. Barnes, stopping him, "but I doubt that the police will believe you any more than they did Connie."

"OK," said the man with a smile, "we will show them. Then they'll *have* to believe it. Come on, Chico, we're going to the police station. And you two must come along."

Mr. Barnes and Connie climbed into the back seat of the sports car. Mr. Barnes squeezed his daughter's hand. "I'm sorry I didn't believe you before, dear," he said. "Next time I promise to trust you—no matter what monkey business you get into!"

As they drove to the station, the man, whose name was Enrico the Great, explained why Chico drove the car.

"The idea is to get people's attention," he said. "Then they will be curious enough to come to the circus. That's where Chico and I work."

"Does Chico drive a car in the circus?" Connie wanted to know.

Enrico the Great laughed. "No," he replied. "The circus owner thinks it's too dangerous."

As they pulled into the police station, two officers in a car saw them. The driver was startled by the sight of Chico driving. He nearly drove right up on the grass.

"Well, I'm glad to see I'm not the only person upset to see a monkey in the driver's seat!" laughed Connie.

Worth His Weight in . . .

"LOOK AT THAT CAT," said Alice to her cousin Arlene. Doesn't he ever do anything useful? What good is a fat cat that sits in front of the fireplace all day? He doesn't even notice we're here."

"Don't talk like that in front of King Tomcat," answered Arlene. "He knows we're here. He just doesn't choose to care.

"You never can tell. He might turn out to be a great watchcat some day"...

WORTH HIS WEIGHT IN...

That's all. He knows you're not a cat person. And he does more than sit in front of the fire."

"Like what?" asked Alice. "At least the dog barks at me once in a while. That cat does nothing."

"Not so," said Arlene. "You just don't like cats. King Tomcat catches mice and. . . ."

"And birds," said Alice before Arlene could finish. "But what does he do that's helpful?"

"You never can tell. He might turn out to be a great watchcat some day," answered Arlene. "Just like Blackjack, his father."

"A watchcat? What on earth is that? A cat that tells time?" kidded Alice. "Come on, Arlene. If you bought a mousetrap you wouldn't need King Tom at all. Cats are useless. Face it."

"No they're not. Blackjack wasn't useless. He lived at the bank where my mother used to work," said Arlene. "Once he saved the bank a lot of money."

"I suppose you're going to tell me that Blackjack was a watchcat," said Alice.

"That's right," answered Arlene. "And a very good one too."

"I don't believe it," said Alice. "All that money and the bank used a cat to watch it? You've got to be kidding."

"No, I'm not kidding. That cat lived in the bank. He was there to catch mice," Arlene told Alice. "He ended up saving the bank nearly half a million dollars. I'll tell you all about it. . . ."

Here's what Arlene told Alice:

Blackjack was a big, beautiful, black cat. He lived in the City Bank. Most of the people who banked there knew Blackjack. The cat often sat right on the bank manager's desk. Sometimes he sat on the counter next to the money. Sometimes he walked around.

One day a man opened a new account in the bank. His name was Jim Roberts. He came into the bank each week. Each week he put a little money in the account. Each week he looked things over very carefully. Sometimes he saw Blackjack. When he did, he reached down and scratched the cat's ears.

People thought Jim Roberts was in the bank to put money in his account. He was, but that wasn't all. He had something else in mind. Putting money in his account was just an excuse to get into the bank. Roberts was planning a bank robbery. When he was in the bank, he was busy looking things over.

Jim noticed where the television cameras were. He figured out how to turn them off. He found each of the bank's alarms. He figured out how to turn them off too.

Jim started to work on the lock.

WORTH HIS WEIGHT IN...

Jim found the way to the bank's safe. He wanted to go where the big money was. He was very clever as he planned things. No one knew what was on his mind.

At last Jim was ready. He hid in the bank at closing time on a Friday. When everyone had gone home, Jim went to work. He turned off the television cameras. He turned off each alarm. He waited a while to be sure everything was quiet. Then he went to the safe. All the money was locked in the safe for the weekend.

Jim started to work on the lock. It was a combination lock. To open it, each dial had to be turned to the right numbers. He had a very good sense of touch. His fingers seemed to know just how to turn the dials. Jim knew he could figure it out. He was an expert at opening locks.

Jim turned the dial on the door one

BUGS, SNAKES AND CREEPY THINGS

way. Then he turned it the other way. He listened carefully. At last he heard the lock click. He had figured out the first part of the combination. Then again he turned the dial. And he listened. Finally he got the rest of it. The heavy door swung open.

Slowly Jim went in. He had turned off all the alarms, but he wanted to be sure. Nothing happened. He walked a bit further. He began to feel like a rich man. The money was there. Piles and piles of it.

He began to put the money into a bag. "Hello, Blackjack," he said as he reached down to touch the cat. "What are you doing here at this hour?"

Blackjack walked quietly to the door. As Jim reached once more for the cat, the door began to swing shut. Jim had leaned on it. Blackjack must have pushed it a little too. It swung slowly. Jim was busy counting his cash. He paid it no mind.

WORTH HIS WEIGHT IN...

The heavy door shut all the way.

Jim's bag was full of bills. He was a happy man. Then he tried to leave. There was one big problem. The inside of the door had no handle. Jim was locked in. There was no way to get out.

Jim looked at the alarm button. He knew he was caught. "I'll get it over with," he said to himself. "They've got me now." He pushed the button. Nothing happened. Nothing was going to happen either. Jim had cut all the wires to the alarm.

"Now I've really done it," said Jim. He began to yell. No one heard him through the thick door. No one was there to hear him. Blackjack didn't even meow.

It was late Friday night. No one would show up at the bank until Monday morning. Jim was scared. He was cold and thirsty.

When the bank manager opened the

Blackjack walked up and down the hall, as if nothing had happened. The cat just wanted his dish of milk.

vault on Monday morning, he got quite a surprise. Jim Roberts was curled up near the door. He had nearly died trying to get out. The air had almost been used up. Jim knew he would go to jail, but he was glad to be alive.

Blackjack walked up and down the hall as if nothing had happened. The cat just wanted his dish of milk.

"That's quite a story," said Alice. "Are you sure King Tomcat is Blackjack's son? How did you get him?"

"That's another story, Alice," said Arlene. "But I'm sure Blackjack is Tom's father. Maybe someday our cat will do something brave. Maybe he'll get his picture in the paper too."

"Don't hold your breath, Arlene," said Alice. "I think King Tomcat would rather sit by the fire."

Before the Earth Moved

"DENNIS, LOOK AT Dandy. There's something wrong with that dog. He seems very strange," said Polly. Her voice sounded a bit shaky. "It scares me a little. I wonder what's the matter with him. Go downstairs and take a look at him."

"Nothing's the matter," said Polly's brother Dennis, without looking away from the television. "He's just a little crazy, that's all. Why shouldn't he be? He just takes after his owners."

"Come on, Dennis. Stop kidding me," Polly said. Her voice was getting louder. "Dandy's just not acting right. Please take a look at him. Please, Dennis."

"During half time, OK? I'm not going to get up from a great game to look at a crazy dog," snapped Dennis. "You should know better than to ask. Now leave me alone and let me watch my game in peace."

"You'd think there was nothing in the world but football," Polly said, even though she knew Dennis wasn't listening. "Every Sunday is the same. No one can get you to do anything until the game is over."

"I give up," said Polly. "I'll have to get help from someone else." She went to the telephone and dialed her friend, Ron. Ron wasn't happy. He hated the phone to ring during a good football game.

"Hello, Ron," said Polly. "What are you doing?"

"What do you think I'm doing?" answered Ron. He didn't sound happy. "It's Sunday afternoon. Isn't everyone watching the game? What's Dennis doing? I bet he's not talking on the telephone."

"I know you're watching the game," said Polly. "But I called to find out what your dogs are doing. Are they acting right?"

Ronnie was quiet for a second. "That's a funny thing to ask, Polly," he said. "What made you come up with a question like that?"

"Just answer me," said Polly. "Then I'll tell you why I asked."

"Well, the truth is," said Ron, "my dogs *are* acting a little crazy. How did you know that? You live on the other side of town. You couldn't hear them barking all

"... something strange is happening. Our animals are acting a bit crazy."

the way over there."

"I didn't know your dogs were barking," said Polly. "But my dog is really strange. He's running around and barking. He hasn't eaten anything today. He just keeps running from one window to another. He will not stay out in the yard. He keeps wanting to come into the house. I think he's sick."

"My dogs won't keep quiet either. They just keep howling. When I went out to see what was wrong," said Ron, "Kaynine almost bit me. She's never done that before. Houndog just growled."

"Something strange is going on here," said Polly, "and I'm scared. The dogs must know something we don't."

"Don't be silly, Polly," laughed Ronnie. "How can dogs know anything humans don't? But I agree that something strange is happening. Our animals are acting a bit crazy."

"What should we do, Ron?" asked Polly. "We should do something. Dennis isn't any help. He just made the television louder and told me to leave him in peace."

"I'm going to call Joe," said Ron. "I'll ask him how his animals are. He's got so many of them. If his are going crazy, too, we'll know we've got something here."

Joe's phone rang and rang. At last he answered. "Joe here," he said. "What is it? Hurry, I gotta run."

"Hello, Joe. This is Ron. What's happening?"

"No time to talk, Ron," answered Joe. "I'm having problems with the animals. The dogs keep trying to bring the sheep in. I can't control them. They've moved all my sheep from the big field on the hill. Now I've got two hundred sheep in the barnyard and three crazy sheepdogs. Something is wrong. My animals are acting strange. The sheep are making a lot of noise. They keep milling around and they won't eat the grass."

"That's why I called, Joe," said Ron. "My dogs are going wild too. Polly's dog is frantic. Now you tell me your dogs just brought in all the sheep. What's going on?"

"I wish I knew," answered Joe. "It isn't time for a full moon. The weather is nice. It seems like any other day. But these crazy animals are telling us something. . . ."

"It's really a puzzle," said Ron. "I wonder what's going on."

"Thanks for calling, Ron," said Joe. "If I figure out anything, I'll let you know."

"Right," Ron answered. "By the way, are you going to Cindy's party tonight?"

"No," answered Joe. "I don't dare leave the farm now. Not with the animals acting like this. Besides, it's too long a drive into the city for me. Remember, I don't live as close as you do."

"That's too bad, Joe," said Ron. "We'll miss you. Give me a ring tomorrow. Let me know how things are going."

When Ron got off the phone, his dogs were still barking. They wouldn't sit still. Ronnie started to get ready for the party. At seven o'clock he drove over to pick up Polly and Dennis.

"How's it going?" Ron asked.

"Bad game today," answered Dennis. "And that dog never quieted down."

"C'mon, we've got to get going. We're going to be late," said Polly. "We'll just have to leave the crazy dog here."

The three of them started to walk toward the door. Suddenly, the house began to shake. Some cups and a bowl fell off the shelf and broke into little pieces. The lamp fell off Polly's desk. A

Suddenly, the house began to shake.

few pictures fell off the walls. The dog ran under the bed.

"It's the end of the world," said Polly. "I knew it!"

"Turn on the radio," said Ron. "Let's find out what's going on."

"An earthquake has just hit the San Francisco Bay area," said a voice on the radio. "We don't know yet how bad it is. Reports are already coming in. Stay off the streets and wait for further word. We'll bring you details as soon as we have them."

"An earthquake!" screamed Polly. "Those animals were trying to tell us something. They knew all the time. I wonder how they could tell."

"I don't know," said Dennis. "But they sure knew something was happening. I wonder what Joe's sheep are doing now? Too bad this didn't happen during the game. They'd have had to call it off.

"An earthquake has just hit the San Francisco Bay area"...

Then maybe our team would get another chance."

The voice on the radio went on. "The earthquake was a bad one. We've got ten reports from north of the city. Many people have told us they've been having trouble with their animals today. Dogs have been barking. Horses and cattle have been running around. Animals have not been eating. One man in the city said that his pet frogs were croaking all day. It proves what some scientists have told us: animals can predict earthquakes. . . ."

"All you have to do is listen to them," Polly said to Dennis. "Come on, let's get this mess cleaned up."

Star of The Show

SANDY DIDN'T have a good home when he was young. He nearly died. No one wanted him around. But he got over his early troubles. He was lucky and went on to become famous.

Sandy became active in the theater. He became quite a good actor. He did very well in his first show. It didn't take long before Sandy became a star.

For Sandy, the great American dream came true. He began with nothing, but he worked very hard. And he became rich enough to have everything he needed and more. Sandy's story is one of rags to riches. And there's one important fact about Sandy that you should know. Sandy isn't a person. He is a dog. Here's how a poor mutt became a top dog.

Bill Berloni, Sandy's owner, had always wanted to be an actor. A few summers ago, a theater near where Bill lived was doing the play *Annie*. It was based on the comic strip *Little Orphan Annie*. The girl in the comic strip had a dog. So, the people doing the show needed a dog to play the part. Bill said he'd help them out.

Bill didn't have Sandy then. But he told them he'd find the right dog. He went out to look for one.

Bill had always liked animals. He grew

"*A few summers ago, a theater near where Bill lived was doing the play Annie.*"

up on a farm. When Bill was very young, his mother asked him if he wanted a brother or sister. "A dog," was Bill's firm answer to that question.

So finding a dog was something Bill didn't mind doing. The dog he needed had to be very ordinary. It had to be of medium size—not too big, and not too little. And it had to be sandy—yellowish—in color.

Bill went to animal shelters. He looked hard for just the right dog. Some were too big. Some were too small. Most were not the right color. At last he found the right one. It was medium-sized. It was sandy in color, and no one knew for sure what kind of a dog it was.

It was sitting in the corner of a cage. It looked very sad. "What's wrong with it?" Bill asked.

"That dog is on the list to be put to sleep," said a worker in the dog pound.

"That dog is on the list to be put to sleep."

STAR OF THE SHOW

"No one seems to want him. We can't find a home for him."

"When do you plan to do that?" Bill asked.

"Tomorrow," answered the worker. "If you want him, you can have him. You just have to pay for the license. Then you can take him away."

And that's how Sandy's life in the theater began. After that summer, the play *Annie* opened on Broadway in New York. People came from all over to see the play, and tickets were very hard to get. Sandy was one of the stars. Everyone loved him and he was a great hit.

Sandy did so well, that Bill began to worry. *What would happen if Sandy got sick?* he thought. *How could the show go on without Sandy? We'd better get another dog just in case. The show must go on.*

So, Bill went back to the pound to find

another dog and he found Arf. Arf needed a home. He was medium size. No one knew what kind of dog he was. And he seemed friendly. He became the understudy for Sandy. Sandy never got sick, so no one knew how Arf would do on the stage. He never got the chance to fill in for Sandy. But he was ready.

Arf and Sandy both lived in Bill's apartment in New York. They traveled to and from the theater in a taxi.

One night after the show, some people stopped and asked for Sandy's autograph. "That dog was just great," said one young woman. "May I have his autograph? He was the star of the show."

"Of course," said Bill. "Sandy would be glad to sign your paper for you. Hold it over here."

Sandy put his paw on an ink pad. Then he put it on the paper. The woman went away happy. She had the autograph of

*One night after the show, some people stopped
and asked for Sandy's autograph.*

the show's star.

Then Sandy and Arf got into their taxi. They were glad the show was over for the night. They wanted to go home.

Dan's Big Dance

"WHOEVER HEARD OF A DANCE where nobody dances?" said Dan Tyler.

The members of Maple High's Freshman Student Council looked up at their president's troubled face. No one said a word.

"Every time we have a dance here at school everyone ends up just standing around," continued Dan.

"That's not true," said Lorie Hughes. "Lots of the girls dance."

"Yes," Dan agreed. "But they dance with each other!"

"So what's wrong with that?" asked Lorie.

"*Everything!*" boomed Dan. "It would be better if they didn't dance at all!"

Tom Ramon shook his head and smiled. "You know how most of the guys in our class are, Dan," he said. "They'd rather face a month of staying after school than dance with a girl."

"That's only because they don't know *how* to dance," Dan said.

"So what is there to dancing?" piped up Suzie Lu Won. "All you have to do is wave your arms and feet to the music. Even my five-year-old brother can do *that*."

"Maybe we should ask your brother

DAN'S BIG DANCE

and his friends to come to the dance," joked Tom.

Dan stood up. "Well, jokes aside, I don't see any point in continuing to hold freshman dances if most of the girls are going to just stand around and a lot of the guys are going to be in the gym shooting baskets."

What Dan was saying was true. Some of the boys headed straight for the gym the minute they got to the dances. They only came back to the dance floor to load up on refreshments. It was something no one liked to admit.

Finally Lorie spoke up. "But we have to do *something* with the money put aside for school dances!"

"Come on, Dan," said Tom. "Be reasonable about this. We *have* to have a dance."

"OK," Dan said at last. "We'll have a spring dance for the freshman class. Just

"Come on, Dan... Be reasonable about this. We have to have a dance."

DAN'S BIG DANCE

like Maple High has every year. Only this year it's going to be a *real* dance. Not girls with girls, but boy-girl, boy-girl!"

"How do you plan to do that?" asked Suzie. "Handcuff them together?" Everyone laughed at that.

"You just leave that to me," answered Dan firmly. "I'll find a way if it's the last thing I do as class president!"

That night after dinner, Dan told his parents about what happened in school.

"Maybe you're being too hard on the boys," said his mother. "After all, they still have three years of high school to discover that a young lady's company can be fun."

"That's not the point," Dan insisted. "Dancing can be as much fun as shooting baskets or anything else. They just haven't given it a chance."

Mr. Tyler looked up from his evening

paper. "I remember the first dance I ever went to," he said. "On one side of the hall sat the girls and on the other side sat the boys. In the center of the room was Mrs. Prindle, an old, tough teacher. She would sit by the band—we didn't have many records back in those days—and keep time to the music with a twelve-inch wooden ruler."

"So what happened?" asked Dan.

"Within fifteen minutes every chair on the sidelines would be empty," explained his father. "We all decided that dancing with a girl was less painful than a good taste of Mrs. Prindle's ruler."

"How old were you when that happened?" Dan wanted to know.

"Oh, seventeen, I think," said Mr. Tyler.

"I guess kids developed a lot slower back in those days, eh, Dad?" grinned Dan.

DAN'S BIG DANCE

"One more remark like that, young man," replied his father smiling, "and I may start looking for a good, stiff ruler myself!"

The night of the Maple High Freshman "Spring Fling" was warm and breezy. Dan, Lorie, and Tom were in the cafeteria early setting up for the dance.

"I have to hand it to you, Dan," said Lorie. "You've really put everything into making this night a success."

"That doesn't mean it *will* be a success," said Tom.

"And I say the only action you're going to see here tonight will be on the gym floor," said Tom.

Dan smiled at him. "Would you like to bet money on that?"

Tom took three one dollar bills from his pocket and flashed them before Dan's eyes. "This says the Spring Fling flops," he said.

"You're on," replied Dan, taking out his own money. "Lorie, you hold the bets."

"I'll say this much for you, Dan Tyler," said Lorie, "you don't lack confidence."

Pretty soon the cafeteria began to fill up with young people. The girls had on brightly colored dresses. The boys wore their best clothes and shoes. When Dan thought the time was right, he turned on the record player. He played a fast song with a strong beat. It was just the thing to get feet tapping.

Suddenly a cry came from one end of the cafeteria. "Hey! What's going on?" shouted a boy named George.

"Something wrong?" asked Dan, as he quickly crossed the floor.

"I'll say there is!" exclaimed George. "The gym's locked. We can't get in!"

"Let's give it to him!" George cried.

"So what?" said Dan. "The dance is in here. Not in the gym."

A group of angry boys began to gather around Dan. "Don't be wise," said George. "You know we always shoot baskets in the gym during dances."

"Well," smiled Dan, "it looks like this dance is going to be a little different, doesn't it?"

The boys began to close in on Dan. "Let's give it to him!" George cried.

"Break it up!" spoke an older voice. It was Mr. Morgan, a teacher.

"Dan's right," Mr. Morgan said. "A dance is no place for basketball. Now get back in here. All of you. Or go home."

Dan was glad to see Mr. Morgan. He just saved him from a bad fight. But if Dan thought locking the gym would get the dance moving, he was mistaken.

"Well, you put an end to team sports for the evening," admitted Tom. "But I

DAN'S BIG DANCE

don't see any mixed couples on the dance floor."

It was true. A few pairs of girls were moving around to the music. The others were sitting on the sidelines. A few of the braver boys were talking to a few of the girls. But only talking.

Dan turned to Tom. "I've just begun to fight!" he said.

Dan spotted his friend Sam sitting alone. He quickly walked over to him. "Come on, Sam," Dan said. "Let's get out there and show these other guys how to dance."

Sam looked like an animal caught in a trap. "I don't think I can right now, Dan," he replied.

"But don't you see?" explained his friend. "Once you start everyone will join in."

Sam looked doubtful. "How do you know that?" he asked. "Maybe I'll just end up making a fool of myself."

Dan sighed and worked on his other friends. One said he had an upset stomach. Another said he didn't like the music they were playing. A third claimed to have hurt his foot in gym class. Everyone had an excuse not to dance. Things were looking bad for Dan—and his three dollar bet.

Just then Lorie came up to him. "The pizza's just about ready, Dan," she told him. "Can we put it out on the tables yet?"

Dan looked at her and a strange gleam came into his eyes.

"Is something wrong?" Lorie asked.

"No, everything's just fine!" exclaimed Dan. "Thanks to you and the idea you just gave me!"

Dan's parents arrived at the school dance about ten.

DAN'S BIG DANCE

"I hope he doesn't mind us showing up like this without telling him," said his mother.

"Of course he won't," said his father, as they walked into the cafeteria. "He'll be glad to have our support if this dance is as bad as I think—"

Mr. Tyler was stopped short. The dance floor was packed with dancing couples.

"I don't believe it!" said Mr. Tyler.

"How did he ever do it?" wondered his wife.

"Hi, Mr. and Mrs. Tyler!" called out a voice from the dance floor. It was Sam. He was dancing with a cute blonde. "Great dance, isn't it?" he said.

"It certainly is, Sam," answered Mrs. Tyler. "Tell me, how—" But Sam didn't hear. He had more important things on his mind and the music was too loud.

The older people pushed their way

through the dancing bodies. Suddenly they saw Tom standing by himself.

"Tom," said Mr. Tyler, "you must be about the only fellow who isn't out there dancing."

"I guess so, Mr. Tyler," replied Tom. "When a guy loses a week's allowance in a bet he doesn't feel much like partying."

"How did you lose it, Tom?" asked Mrs. Tyler with concern.

"By thinking I could outsmart that son of yours," he said. "See you folks around."

Dan's parents looked at each other. "This gets more mysterious by the minute!" cried Mr. Tyler. Just then they spotted Lorie coming toward them.

"Hi there!" Lorie said. "What do you think of our Spring Fling?"

"It's great," said Mr. Tyler. "But tell us, how in the world did Dan—" At that moment the record being played ended.

"Oh, excuse me," broke in Lorie. "But I'm needed in the kitchen about now. See you later!"

As she hurried off, Mrs. Tyler pointed to a spotlight in the middle of the dance floor. Dan was standing on it. He was holding up his hands for everyone to quiet down.

"You've all been very good tonight," he said loudly. "I think I can safely say this is the most successful freshman dance that our school has ever had. Now I think we're all ready for some refreshments."

At that, the young people let out a loud cheer. Lorie and Mr. Morgan started putting out pizza and soft drinks. The dancers got to the food and began eating at once. Dan saw his parents and hurried over to them.

"Well, I did it," he said brightly. "Just like I said I would!"

"Yes, Dan," said his mother. "We can

see that. But HOW?"

"Well," smiled Dan, "it was really very easy. I just told them there wouldn't be any food until every guy had danced with a girl. Something must have clicked then, because that was nearly an hour ago!"

Dan's father laughed. "It's just like your mother always said—the quickest way to a man's heart is through his stomach."

Dan grinned. "I guess that goes for their feet, too!" he said.